Flowers in Paris

Flowers in Paris - Coloring Book for Adults

ISBN: 9798863414027

Bonjour!

Flowers in Paris blossomed from many adventures exploring flower shops across Paris. Each charming hand-drawn scene, bouquet, mandala and quote seeks to evoke the allure of adorable bouquets and clever Parisian displays.

Coloring has been proven to relax and calm the mind and provides a wonderful and accessible way to express your creativity.

Have fun choosing color palettes and tools such as colored pencils, crayons, fine-tipped markers or even watercolors.

A word of advice — while a light hand with any water-based media is suggested, please note that water-based paints are likely to make the paper buckle. We've provided a page at the back of the book to experiment on. Also, please note that some markers will bleed through the paper, so we suggest placing a piece of card stock or several sheets of copier paper between the pages to prevent this.

Share your finished work with us on Instagram! Please use #InnerInkColoring and tag us @InnerInkPublishing

www.InnerInkPublishing.com

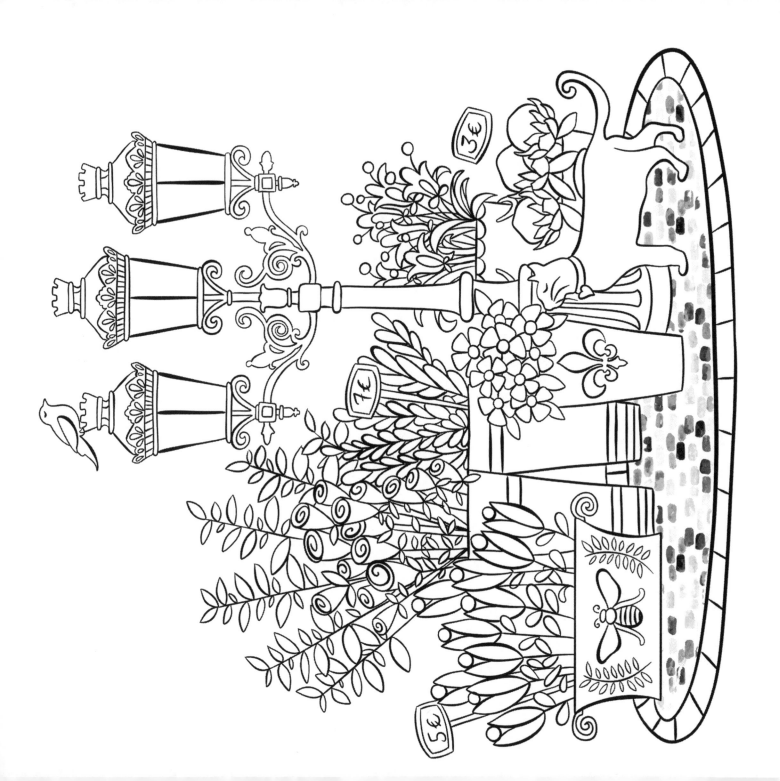

Paris
is
always
a good
idea

4€

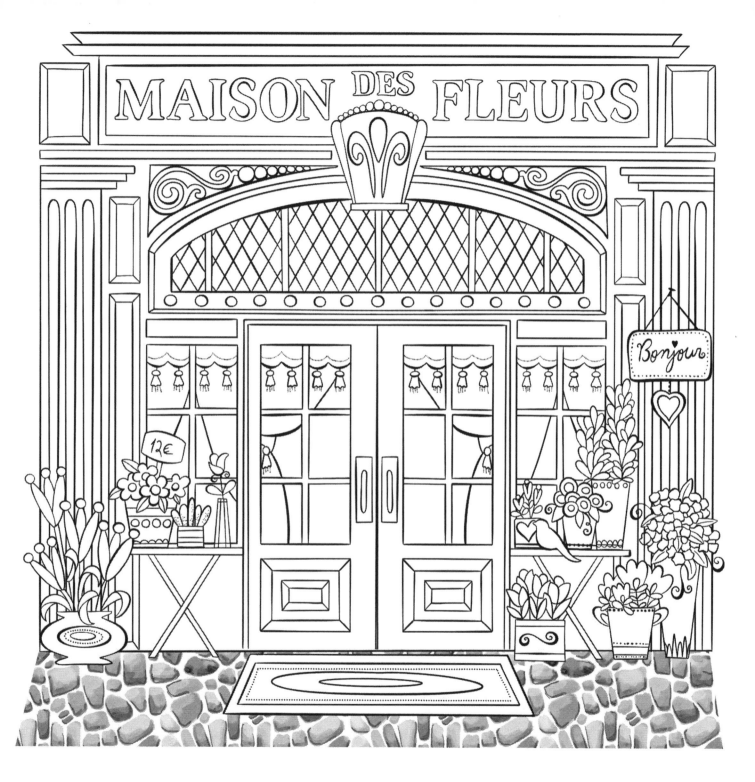

Experiment Here

Merci!

We here at Inner Ink Publishing want to thank you for choosing

Flowers in Paris

We hope that you had fun coloring and that it brought you some inner peace :-)

If you enjoyed this book we'd be so grateful if you'd leave a review on Amazon.
https://bit.ly/FlowersInParis

And yes! Even if you received Flowers in Paris as a gift, you can leave a review!
We're always open to suggestions on how to improve our books
as well as ideas for books YOU want.
Contact us at innerinkpublishing@gmail.com

As a little gift from us to you, please visit www.InnerInkPublishing.com
to download two beautiful, **FREE coloring pages** and sign up
for a new free coloring page each month.
Just our way of saying Merci!

We'd love to see your finished work!
If you post on Instagram, please use the hashtag:
#innerinkcoloring and tag us @innerinkpublishing

Happy Coloring!

Made in United States
Orlando, FL
15 November 2023

38999739R00046